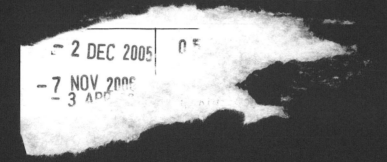

THE FIRST WORLD WAR

Dennis Hamley

W

FRANKLIN WATTS
LONDON•SYDNEY

Designer Jason Anscomb
Editors Constance Novis, Penny Clarke
Art Director Jonathan Hair
Editor-in-Chief John C. Miles
Picture Research Diana Morris

© 2002 Franklin Watts

First published in 2002
by Franklin Watts
96 Leonard Street
London
EC2A 4XD

Franklin Watts Australia
45-51 Huntley Street
Alexandria
NSW 2015

ISBN 0 7496 4436 2

Dewey classification: 940.3

A CIP catalogue record for this book is available
from the British Library.

Printed in Belgium

PHOTOGRAPHIC CREDITS
Front cover: AKG London (main and lower left), Christopher F.
Seidler (middle right), Franklin Watts/Steve Shott (top left, lower
right), Peter Newark's Military Pictures (middle left)
Back cover: AKG London (inset), Peter Newark's Military Pictures
(background)

AKG London: 12t, 16b, 17c, 18c, 19b, 24b, 26-27, 32b, 34, 43b
Corbis: 36-37
Franklin Watts/Steve Shott: 9b, 13b, 39t
Hulton Getty: 7, 23r
Peter Newark's Military Pictures: 2-3, 8b, 9t, 10b, 11b, 15b, 17b, 20b,
21b, 22t, 25t, 28l, 30-31, 38b, 40b, 42b
Christopher F. Seidler: 5b, 14b, 33, 35t

*Whilst every effort has been made to clear copyright should there be an inadvertent
omission the copyright holder should apply to the publisher in the first instance with
a view to rectification.*

CONTENTS

The war that began in 1914 happened almost by accident, yet it had been coming for many years. In Britain, France and Russia, people seemed to know who the impending war would have to be fought against – GERMANY.

Why Germany? Because Germany was a new country. Once it had been a collection of large states, such as Prussia, Bavaria and Saxony, and tiny ones, called duchies, like Hanover.

Germany unified

By 1871 the Prussian Chancellor, Count Otto von Bismarck, had united the German states into a single nation. The new country was strong, with industries and a huge army. In 1870 it had put that army to the test.

Bismarck stated that the French province of Alsace-Lorraine belonged to Germany, and his army invaded France. The Germans only withdrew after France signed a humiliating peace treaty. By the early 1900s the French wanted revenge.

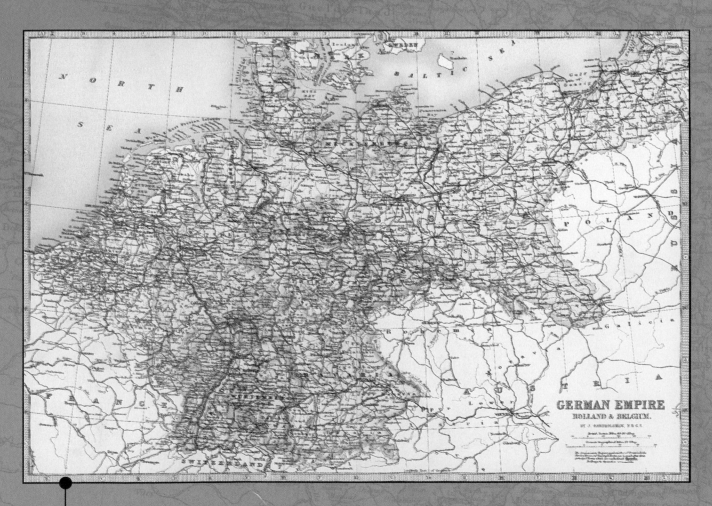

A map of the German Empire from the 1890s.

Britain rules the waves

In the 1800s Britain was the world's strongest power, with a great overseas Empire – India, Canada, Australia, South Africa and many more territories and possessions. This Empire was kept united by a powerful navy – the Royal Navy. Britain was also the first country to develop modern industries, and this had made it rich. But now its people began to fear Germany.

Germany's ambitions

By the late 1800s Germans wanted to be accepted as equal to peoples of the other great nations. Their country's army must be bigger than France's. They wanted an empire like Britain's and to build a fleet to rival the Royal Navy. Most of all, Germans believed they had to make themselves so strong that nobody would dare to attack them.

Rivalry and fear grow

When Germans of the early 1900s looked at the map of Europe, they felt fear and suspicion. Their country was surrounded by enemies. France and Russia had signed a treaty of friendship. Germany could be squeezed to death between the two. And Britain? Who knew what the British would do? Perhaps they were the greatest foe of all.

In Britain and Germany many people prophesied a great war to come, in which the two countries would struggle for world mastery.

Above all, the British people feared a German invasion. What if the many resident Germans – waiters in restaurants, musicians in bands – were really a secret army? What if a hidden German fleet was waiting to cross the North Sea? By 1914 Europe had become a collection of countries eyeing each other with suspicion and fear.

A smart young German soldier poses proudly for an official photograph in about 1910.

WAR COMES

By 1910 the rivalry and fear between European nations had led to a complex web of alliances, or agreements between countries to help each other if war broke out.

Germany's friends

Germany needed friendly nations, or allies, to further its aims. To the south was the German-speaking Austro-Hungarian Empire. Its leader, Franz Joseph, ruled an empire consisting of Austria, Hungary, Czechoslovakia and other Balkan countries including Bosnia.

Here was Germany's natural ally. Other sympathetic countries included Bulgaria and Turkey. Together all these nations became known as the Central Powers.

France, Russia and friends

In 1892 France and Russia had signed a treaty of friendship. If one country were attacked, the other would come to that nation's aid. Britain and France also joined together in an "Entente Cordiale", or friendly agreement, in 1903. This didn't commit Britain to helping France in war – but Britain had signed a separate treaty with Belgium which said that Britain must help that country if it were attacked. All these countries were known as the Allied Powers, or the Allies.

The Schlieffen Plan

German generals were afraid that one day they might have to fight a war on two fronts, one in the east and one in the west. Years earlier Field Marshal von Schlieffen had devised a plan to conquer France in six weeks and then travel quickly east to fight Russia.

The Seed

War broke. And now the winter of the world
With perishing great darkness closes in.
The foul tornado, centred on Berlin,
Is over all the width of Europe whirled,
Rending the sails of progress. Rent or furled
Are all Art's ensigns. Verse moans. Now begin
Famines of thought and feeling. Love's wine's thin.
The grain of human Autumn rots, down-hurled.

For after Spring had bloomed in early Greece,
And Summer blazed her glory out with Rome,
An Autumn softly fell, a harvest home,
A slow grand age, and rich with all increase.
But now, for us, wild Winter, and the need
Of sowings for new Spring, and blood for seed.

Wilfred Owen (1893-1918)

German troops would march through Belgium and take Paris from the north before the French knew what was happening.

The spark that set it all off

In 1914 Bosnia was part of the Austro-Hungarian Empire, but many Bosnians did not want to be. As Slavs, they considered themselves to be part of neighbouring Serbia.

On 28 June 1914 the heir to the Austro-Hungarian Empire, Archduke Franz Ferdinand, and his wife Sophie were on a state visit to Sarajevo in Bosnia. They were assassinated by Gavrilo Princip, a 19-year-old student and supporter of the Serb nationalist Black Hand Gang.

An official greets Archduke Franz Ferdinand and his wife moments before their assassination, 1914.

What next?

Austria, furious, declared war on Serbia. As allies, Germany had to help Austria. Immediately Russia, also a Slav nation, came to Serbia's aid. France was now bound by its treaty to help Russia. This was Germany's chance to put the Schlieffen Plan into operation. But when the German Army entered Belgium, Britain too was brought into the war.

On 4 August 1914, six weeks after Gavrilo Princip fired his fatal shot, all the major countries in Europe were at war.

> "The lamps are going out all over Europe. I doubt if we shall see them lit again in our lifetimes."
> Sir Edward Grey, British Foreign Secretary

THE NATIONS AND THEIR ARMIES

Except for Britain, all the major warring countries were on the mainland of Europe.

Continental armies

Because they had long land borders to guard, the countries of mainland Europe maintained large standing armies in 1914. All men had to do military service for a time. As soon as war was declared, huge reserves of trained soldiers could be called up. France, Germany, Austria and Russia had armies numbering millions.

The British Army

In contrast to this state of affairs, Britain did not possess a huge army.

It had not fought in Europe since the Crimean War 70 years before. Even in the Napoleonic Wars against France it had been stronger at sea than on land. The Battle of Waterloo in 1815 had been won by German as much as by British soldiers.

But Britain was not unprepared for war. It had spent a lot of money on its navy, especially the huge new warships known as "Dreadnoughts". Who needed a peacetime army when the Royal Navy was invincible? Britain's military strategists thought it best to keep a small, efficient army that could travel quickly to trouble spots in the Empire when needed.

Countries all over the British Empire sent soldiers to fight. This is a recruiting poster from Australia.

Australia has promised Britain
50,000 MORE MEN
WILL YOU HELP US KEEP THAT PROMISE

Britain's new army is formed

Lord Kitchener was a British military hero as well as being Chief of the Army General Staff. He realised immediately that France could not be expected to do all the fighting. However, Britain's army was much too small to provide sufficient support. The country needed more soldiers.

In 1914, Kitchener proposed a huge new volunteer army. The call for men went out across the country. Kitchener's face appeared on recruiting posters everywhere (left). At once, thousands of young men joined up with their friends, forming battalions of "Pals" and "Chums" to escape humdrum existences and to fill their lives with patriotic glory.

"WANTS YOU"
JOIN YOUR COUNTRY'S ARMY!
GOD SAVE THE KING

Reproduced by permission of LONDON OPINION

German pre-war military identification passes. All the major countries of mainland Europe maintained large armies.

"It will all be over by Christmas."
What people really believed in August 1914

"God with us" reads the inscription on this German belt buckle. Everyone believed what they were doing was right.

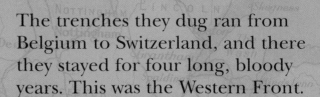

The Germans gave themselves 40 days to conquer France. But the tiny Belgian army slowed the invaders down; for the first time people knew what a terrible war this was going to be.

All the French wanted was Alsace-Lorraine back, and towards it their army marched, as the Germans tried to encircle them. Soon Paris was threatened.

The British arrive

General French's "contemptibly small army", as the Kaiser called the British Expeditionary Force, reached France and fought the Germans at Mons in Belgium on 23 August. During the battle, many thought they saw an angel in the sky. Was this an omen of victory?

Not yet. By bus and taxi, French troops were rushed to the front, and the battle of the Marne took place on 5 September. At last the Schlieffen Plan was defeated.

Now the Allies drove the Germans back until the armies stopped, exhausted, and dug themselves in.

The trenches they dug ran from Belgium to Switzerland, and there they stayed for four long, bloody years. This was the Western Front.

In the East

Meanwhile, in eastern Europe, the Central Powers fought with Russia. The Russians suffered heavy defeats fighting the Germans in 1914. They had more success against the Austro-Hungarian army, which had to be reinforced with Germans in order to survive. The battle front in eastern Europe was long, and armies had to march great distances to fight.

The British Expeditionary Force embarks for France in 1914.

A new kind of war

On the Western Front the dug-in trench warfare was a new way of fighting. Previously wars had been long advances and retreats, decisive battles with winners and losers. But once the armies entrenched, they were stuck. All they could fight over was the devastated ground between their trenches – no-man's land.

By the end of 1914 a new pattern emerged. First came bombardment by the artillery, then the infantry climbed out of the trenches to advance on the enemy's trenches. One or twice they captured them. Usually they were mown down by the machine guns of the defenders.

The Germans usually dug in deep on high ground and fortified their trenches well, aiming to grind the Allies down. The Allies wanted one great breakthrough to take them all the way to Berlin. They never got it.

Christmas 1914

At Christmas that year on the Western Front, German and British soldiers stopped firing. They met in friendship, played football, sang carols and talked as friends. Their commanders never allowed this to happen again.

French soldiers slog their way through a muddy trench with an improvised stretcher in 1915; one of their comrades lies dead.

LIFE IN THE TRENCHES

Has humanity ever endured such misery before or since?

The German trenches were deep and often lined with concrete. Bringing in new supplies was easy – just a short railway journey. For the Allies, especially the British with the English Channel between them and home, things were more difficult.

Water everywhere

The land in Belgium and Northern France is low lying. When soldiers dug trenches they soon hit water. Trenches flooded, became seas of mud and had to be lined with sandbags. Soon the soldiers' socks and boots were soaked. With no chance of dry ones, soldiers got a crippling disease known as "trench foot", which caused as many casualties as enemy fire. Their uniforms were infested with lice. Rats stole their rations, unless they were killed and eaten first. And always soldiers were sniped at, bombarded, repelling raiding parties, burying their dead, renewing the barbed wire barriers between them and the enemy, in constant danger of death.

Units could spend weeks at a time in the front-line trenches before being relieved for a few days' break and a chance to get some sleep.

Trenches were constructed with a parapet of sandbags to give cover to soldiers, as shown in this French postcard.

What were the trenches like?

Trenches were dug as deep as possible – men had to fight, eat, sleep and stay alive in them. There was a ridge along the front, the firestep, so snipers could see over the sandbag parapet and soldiers could "go over the top" (leap out) more easily when they had to attack.

Trenches were never dug in straight lines, otherwise an enemy machine gunner could stand at one end, fire down the trench and kill everyone in it. Instead they were a zig-zag maze. Leading out of the main trenches into the middle of no-man's land were straight trenches called "saps". Here sentries kept watch all night.

Soldiers slept in "dug-outs" at the back of the trench. Leading into the trench from behind were trenches for communications; further back were trenches where troops would wait before taking over the front line.

Trench raids

Sometimes parties of soldiers volunteered to make night raids on enemy trenches. They took knives, clubs and home-made bombs as well as rifles, bayonets and Mills bombs (hand grenades). Their aim was to kill as many of the enemy as they could. These were dangerous operations; very often few of the raiders returned.

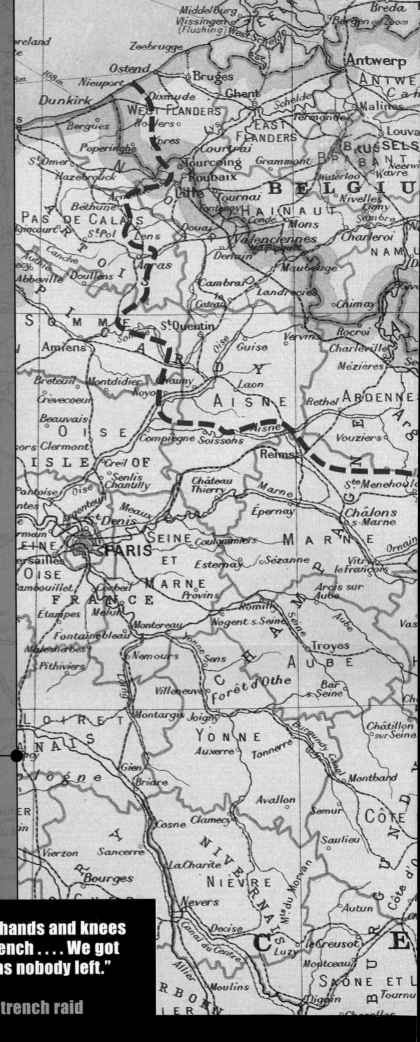

The extent of the front-line trenches in Belgium and northern France, 1916.

Bayonet designed to fit on the end of a German Mauser rifle.

"I just crawled on my hands and knees and got back in the trench . . . . We got annihilated. There was nobody left."

A soldier describes a trench raid

NEW WEAPONS OF WAR

The Industrial Revolution of the 19th century had paved the way for the invention of new, mass-produced ways of waging war. These had a major impact on the way the First World War was fought.

Barbed wire

Tangled coils of barbed wire, sometimes over twenty metres wide, provided barriers to the trenches. Advancing troops, leaping over the top to attack the other side, needed gaps cut in their own barbed wire and then had to cut a way through the enemy's. Gunfire before the attack was supposed to destroy the wire, but somehow it never did. Thousands of men died tangled in the wire as machine-gun fire tore into them while they tried to cut a way through.

Machine guns

In May 1915 General Sir Douglas Haig, soon to be British Commander-in-Chief, told the War Council, "The machine gun is a much over-rated weapon." He thought that two for each company were quite enough. The Germans made no such mistake.

They realised that four men manning two machine guns could mow down hundreds of attacking soldiers. At the Battle of Loos in 1915, massed lines of British soldiers advanced on the German machine-gun positions "offering such a target as had never been seen before".

The Germans called the battle "the Field of Corpses of Loos". Out of respect they refused to fire while the British collected their dead and wounded. The machine gun was the deadliest weapon of all, even more so than...

Machine-gun teams in action in Palestine, 1915.

Gas!

The Germans were the first to use poison gas, which caused lungs to fill up with froth, eyes to go blind, nausea and a lingering, painful death. It worked well unless the wind changed and blew it back on the users. Other armies started using it as soon as they could. But not before efficient respirators were developed.

Aeroplanes

The newest, biggest, most far-reaching advance in the First World War was the development of fighting aircraft. When war broke out, it was only eleven years since the brothers Orville and Wilbur Wright had made the first flight ever. Yet by 1918 the sky was full of efficient fighters and bombers. First, aeroplanes were used for observation. Then aircrew started taking rifles and pistols up with them. Next, machine guns were installed. Pilots who shot down many enemy planes were called "aces", like Englishman Edward Mannock, American Eddie Rickenbacker and German

> "5 September. Today being a holiday, Company Commanders had to go to St Omer to see how to kill our fellow creatures with gas."
>
> **From a British officer's diary**

Count Manfred von Richthofen, the "Red Baron".

Aeroplanes clearly had an important role in future wars. So, in 1918, the British amalgamated the army's Royal Flying Corps and the navy's Royal Navy Air Service to form the Royal Air Force.

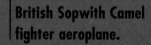

British Sopwith Camel fighter aeroplane.

1915

All through 1915 the Allies were getting nowhere, simply losing men in vain attacks on the German trenches. In the east, war between the Central Powers and Russia swung back and forth. How could this deadlock be broken? Attack Turkey.

A third front

There were many reasons for attacking Turkey. For example, this plan would mean Turkish troops could not fight against Russia. It would stop Germany having an entry to the Middle Eastern oilfields. It would open up a third front, which was something the Central Powers were desperately keen to prevent.

In addition, Australian and New Zealand troops on their way to France could be diverted to secure a quick victory and remove Turkey from the war. The idea could have worked. But indecision, poor communications and a Turkish army far better than anyone expected meant that the landings at Gallipoli in spring 1915 were a disaster.

Thousands of troops, many from Australia and New Zealand, died in the hot weather at Suvla Bay and along the coast. The attack ended in stalemate just like the Western Front. Finally, after ten weary, bloodstained months, the Allied troops were withdrawn. Nothing had been gained but thousands of men had died.

Allied troops swarm out of their trenches at Gallipoli, 1915.

GERMAN WAR IN THE AIR AND AT SEA

Zeppelins

Zeppelins were slow-moving airships filled with hydrogen gas to make them float in the air. They had been developed by the German Count von Zeppelin in the early 1900s and soon they were used to drop bombs.

U-boats, the *Lusitania* and the United States

Britain's navy imposed a sea blockade of Germany, cutting off imported food supplies. Germany feared a sea battle with the Royal Navy – but had other ideas about breaking its power.

German Zeppelin airship.

From August 1914, London and some British east coast towns suffered Zeppelin raids. Compared with the Blitz or RAF raids on Germany in the Second World War, the damage they did was minor. But for the British they were a terrible shock – being an island no longer protected them from the realities of war.

German submarines – U-boats – sank merchant ships and crippled British trade. Sometimes they did more than this. On 7 May 1915 a U-boat torpedoed a British passenger liner, the *Lusitania*, off the coast of Ireland. More than a thousand people drowned; 128 were American.

US President Woodrow Wilson had been trying to keep the USA out of the war. This would surely bring them in. Many Americans thought it should.

1916

1915 had been a terrible year. Something had to end the war. The Central Powers believed they were winning. The Germans thought they knew how to destroy the French army. The Allies thought one great attack would finish the Germans off. 1916 would bring victory – for someone.

First came the greatest artillery bombardment ever seen. Trenches were destroyed, men buried alive. Then came the German infantry. The French fought like tigers to keep them out: more soldiers and guns moved up the *Voie Sacrée* – the Sacred Way – into battle. A new commander, General Philippe Pétain, took over the defence.

A postcard of 1916 showing an idealised French soldier defending Verdun.

Verdun

Verdun was a huge French fortress on the road to Paris. The Germans knew that France would use every soldier it had to defend it. In February the German attack started.

Terrible battles raged, especially round *Mort-Homme* (Dead Man's Hill) and, in the end, the Germans were kept out – *"Ils ne passeront pas."* ("They shall not pass.") At least 700,000 men were killed or wounded.

The Battle of the Somme

This battle, planned as the greatest attack of all time, was supposed to be a joint British-French operation, but as the French were desperate to use every man to defend Verdun, it became mostly British. The plan was to destroy the Germans with a huge artillery bombardment, then the infantry would walk through the destroyed trenches, taking the villages behind the German lines.

Guns and men were brought up to the front. Sadly, the Germans, not half a kilometre away, could see what was happening. Kitchener's army of volunteers was going into action: the battalions of Pals and Chums filed into the trenches.

On the morning of 1 July, after weeks of heavy shelling, the final British bombardment started. Surely nothing could be left alive? At 7.30 am, eleven British divisions – 80,000 men – attacked.

They expected to walk across no-man's land with little opposition. Vain hope. In their deep trenches the Germans had taken cover. They had sat through the furious shelling and were now waiting with machine guns ready. By nightfall 40,000 British soldiers were wounded and 20,000 were dead. It was, and still is, the worst day in the history of the British Army.

All over Britain, whole streets mourned the deaths of husbands, fathers, sons and brothers. Yet somehow, nobody seemed to realise just how bad it was. One newspaper reported, "It is, on balance, a good day for England and France."

"... (the dead) might have been old or young. One could not tell because they had no faces, and were just masses of raw flesh in rags of uniforms ..."

A war correspondent describes the Somme

Exhaustion and fear are etched on the faces of these British soldiers as they wait in their trench at the Battle of the Somme, 1916.

The First Battle of the Somme dragged on all through 1916. It petered out when the Germans, worried about their losses, moved to new positions further east on the famous Hindenburg Line. The British ended up with an advantage, but they couldn't claim to have won it.

Tanks

On 15 September, after months of secret development, a new weapon rolled ponderously into battle. It was called the tank. The British had high hopes of it and for a while the Germans were afraid of it.

Tanks were developed to help men get through the barbed wire and across no-man's land: wirecutters and shells were clearly useless. Equally, there had to be some way of firing guns safely at the enemy and destroying their trenches.

Sadly, the Mark I tank could only travel at a crawl; on rough ground it became completely stuck. But a year later, at the Battle of Cambrai in 1917, an improved version was used. A revolution in fighting battles had begun.

Although armoured, the first tanks were slow and frequently broke down.

War at sea: The Battle of Jutland

People in Britain were sure that the Dreadnoughts of the Royal Navy would win the war. They would smash German sea power and thus their whole war effort. The Germans thought the same of their own High Seas Fleet. Besides, they had to do something break the British blockade. So in May 1916, the German fleet under Admirals Hipper and Scheer set sail. Naval Intelligence warned Admirals Jellicoe and Beatty of this, and the British set out to catch them. They met off the coast of Jutland, Denmark, on 31 May 1916, 259 great warships.

The Germans struck first. HMS *Indefatigable* was sunk; HMS *Queen Mary* blew up. But the Germans were sailing into Admiral Jellicoe's trap, at the mercy of the Dreadnoughts. Admiral Scheer realised: the Germans turned just in time, sinking HMS *Hood* as they went.

The British caught the Germans again, damaging their ships severely. Hipper's flagship, the *Lützow*, was sunk – then, as Scheer ordered his destroyers to start a

mass torpedo attack, Jellicoe ordered the Dreadnoughts away to avoid further damage. Finally, at night, the German fleet escaped home, losing another battleship on the way. They never put to sea again.

Who won the only major sea battle of the war? The Germans sank more ships, but the British were ready for sea again next day. No one risked the great battleships again. Henceforth, Germany's war at sea would be carried out by U-boats.

> **"There's something wrong with our bloody ships today."**
>
> **British Admiral Beatty**

A British battleship in action at Jutland fires its huge guns, 1916.

PATRIOTISM STAYS AT HOME

After two years of war soldiers on all sides thought only of staying alive. They had forgotten the stirring patriotism which had inspired them to join up.

Back at home, where there was no radio or TV and people depended on newspapers, nobody knew what was really going on. They thought that the war was just old-fashioned glamorous battles with clean, painless deaths by bullets or bayonets. Patriotism – "My country right or wrong" – reached great heights of ugliness. In every warring country, hatred for the enemy was stirred up. France and Belgium felt it most deeply – their lands were occupied . In all countries, foreigners, even if they had lived there for years, were interned in case they were spies.

Cowards and conscientious objectors

In Britain, women gave any able-bodied man seen at home not in a uniform a white feather for cowardice. At times they were embarrassingly wrong; the man was wounded and discharged.

In many countries, men objected to the war on conscientious, often religious grounds. As "conscientious objectors", they had to attend

"What did you do in the Great War, Daddy?" is the caption to this British recruiting poster. It was meant to shame men into joining the army.

tribunals to test their genuineness. At first, they too were interned; later they were sent out as medical orderlies or on other non-combatant duties. Perhaps that was best. At home they risked being beaten up.

But when soldiers came home on leave they were often sickened by what they found. They fought their enemies hard – but also respected them because they knew they went through the same hell together and nobody at home understood.

What every family dreaded

Few families got through the war without losing at least one member. First came an official telegram that said "Missing in action".

Then would come a letter from the soldier's commanding officer, giving more details – but often hiding the true facts. Who could bear to know of a husband, father or son dying in agony in a shell-hole, drowning in mud or even being court-martialled and shot for cowardice?

Then would come letters from his comrades. Wouldn't these tell the truth? Very seldom. Soldiers knew their letters would be officially censored and no grieving family ever wanted to receive something half crossed out.

Shot at dawn

Some stories had to wait until the war was over to be told. All warring nations court-martialled and shot their own soldiers for cowardice. The French executed by far the most – thousands were killed after the mutinies of 1917. In Britain, only now are the names of those who were shot being added to war memorials. Nobody understood how human beings reacted under fire and how even the bravest soldier can snap in the end. Nobody knew about shell-shock and nervous breakdowns or that the man who runs away needs help, not a bullet.

Commanders believed that court-martialling and shooting so-called "cowards" set an example to the rest of the army.

There had never been anything like this war. It involved everybody.

Coal had to be mined in huge quantities to keep the railways and navies going. Guns and shells had to be made, ships and aeroplanes built and lorries and tanks produced.

This took organisation. The railways were taken into government control; from now on troop trains and goods trains laden with weapons took precedence over ordinary civilian passenger trains. Passenger ships were requisitioned to take troops to fronts all over the world.

Factories were turned over to war production. For the first time people faced shortages of things they normally took for granted. The war came nearer to home.

Women's work?

All this work would normally be done by the very same able-bodied young men who were now fighting. Who could take their place?

Already, women were doing a lot. Nurses worked in military hospitals both at home and behind the front lines. Women Volunteer Ambulance Drivers, the VADs, did wonderful work transporting the wounded in difficult conditions.

Thousands of women worked in munitions factories in the First World War.
They made shells and bombs and challenged the accepted view of what was "women's work".

Food shortages were common in the warring nations. This picture shows people waiting outside a shop in London that has run out of food.

When the war began, millions of women looked after homes or worked as maids and cooks to rich people. People thought "a woman's place was in the home". Changes came slowly; in Britain, it hadn't been so long ago that riots took place when the first women trained as doctors. Before the war, Suffragettes had campaigned for the right of women to vote in elections. Many men were infuriated; a number of Suffragettes were sent to prison.

But this was war, so in all the warring nations out the women streamed to do "men's work" in the factories making shells and other weapons and operating cranes and machinery. In cities, women drove buses and trams. Some, such as Britons Mairi Chisholm and Elsie Knocker even went to the trenches as front-line nurses.

Changes in society

The war began to change European society forever. Women had made the first breakthroughs into a world previously controlled by men. Women in some countries got the right to vote after the war. But nothing else seemed to change – social unrest and poverty grew. This was worsened by a general feeling that all sacrifices had been in vain. Really profound changes in society had to wait until later in the century.

1917

1916 had been a terrible year. Would 1917 be any better? The German commanders knew that as things stood they would lose. They couldn't go on fighting on two fronts; the German people were on the verge of starvation.

German generals had three objectives: to get Russia out of the war, to keep America out and to starve Britain out with a successful U-boat campaign. But even achieving one of these would help their increasingly difficult position.

The Allies, on the other hand, hoped that yet another great push would succeed where so many others before had failed. After all, in the end, they had more men than the Central Powers. The fact remained that when every German soldier was dead, there would still be some British, French and Russians left.

Whatever happened, something – anything – must happen to end the war in 1917. Otherwise, people in many countries seriously believed that it would never, ever end.

Crowds take to the streets of Petrograd during the chaos of the 1917 Russian Revolution.

The Eastern Front

While the war on the Western Front was, quite literally, stuck in the mud, on the Eastern Front the war ranged from the Balkans and Poland through to the Ukraine and western Russia. Germany and Austria-Hungary gained allies in Bulgaria and Turkey: the Russians were fighting virtually alone. Their army suffered from huge shortages of weapons and, often, poor leadership. But what they did have was men, millions and millions of them.

How the German generals longed to have Russia out of the war! Little did they realise just how close they were to achieving this. Why? Russia was on the point of revolution.

The Bolsheviks, or Communists, were gaining strength – the result of years of unrest among the workers – and matters were coming to a head.

The Russian Revolution

In March 1917 the revolutionary Vladimir Lenin and some Bolshevik friends were allowed to return from exile. As news of his homecoming spread, discontent in the country increased. By December, the Russian Revolution had been successful and the Tsar overthrown. Lenin and Leon Trotsky, the new Russian leaders, signed an armistice with the Central Powers; Germany's two-front nightmare was over.

AMERICA JOINS IN

American troops march through London on their way to the battlefields of France on 15 August 1917.

President Wilson had kept the USA out of the war for three years, despite American anger over the *Lusitania* tragedy.

However, Germany still feared the USA would enter the war. In 1917 Germany's Foreign Minister, Arthur Zimmermann, had a scheme to ensure that no US soldiers came to Europe. Why not get Mexico, with German and Japanese help, to invade the USA and tie up their army?

The Zimmermann telegram

On 17 January 1917, British codebreakers intercepted a secret telegram from Zimmermann to the President of Mexico outlining his plan. President Wilson was shown the telegram. Although many said it was a forgery, it persuaded the President to change his mind. In April, the USA declared war on the Central Powers. Soon the first US troops were crossing the Atlantic.

What about the U-boats?

Germany's submarine campaign wasn't working as well as its leaders hoped. For the first time in the war, merchant ships crossed the Atlantic in convoys escorted by warships and the U-boats actually sank fewer ships.

Mutinies and anti-war feeling

Anti-war feeling was spreading among armies. Russian soldiers mutinied. Trouble in the French army was crushed with great difficulty. German sailors also mutinied. Two were shot; a third, as his death sentence was changed to imprisonment, said, "We just wanted to be treated more like human beings." The war had gone on too long. Anti-war feeling rose, even in the army. The British poet, Siegfried Sassoon, resigned his commission after he came home wounded so he could speak out against the war and what men were being expected to endure.

Arras and Vimy Ridge

In April 1917 the Allies launched another attack on the Hindenburg Line. The British advanced at Arras and the Canadians at Vimy Ridge. Both attacks were partly successful, but at huge cost. Although the Canadians made big gains, the Canadian war memorial there bears the names of 11,500 soldiers killed but never identified. The memorial at Arras has the names of over 35,000 unidentified British soldiers, while only 2,400 have graves.

After Arras was over, the French lauched a big attack. They lost 100,000 men. The German machine guns "sprinkled death unhindered, as with a watering can".

Uncle Sam, the personification of America, tries to persuade young men to join up to fight, 1917.

From "Dulce et Decorum Est"

If in some smothering dreams, you too could pace
Behind the wagon that we flung him in,
And watch the white eyes writhing in his face,
His hanging face, like a devil's sick of sin;
If you could hear, at every jolt, the blood
Come gargling from the froth-corrupted lungs,
Obscene as cancer, bitter as the cud
Of vile, incurable sores on innocent tongues –
My friend, you would not tell with such high zest
To children ardent for some desperate glory,
That old lie: Dulce et decorum est
Pro patria mori.

Wilfred Owen (1893-1918)

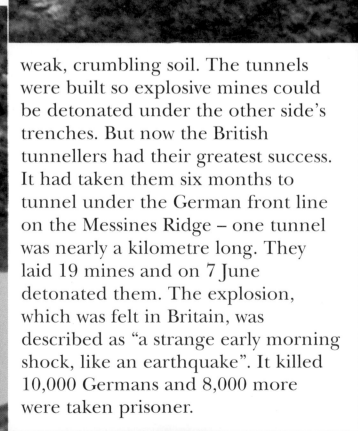

MINES AND MUD

In 1917 there were desperate attempts to break through on the Western Front.

War underground

As war raged in the trenches, another one was taking place underground. Tunnellers were recruited from men who were miners and builders of underground railways. They dug passageways under the earth, sometimes 30 metres deep, often in weak, crumbling soil. The tunnels were built so explosive mines could be detonated under the other side's trenches. But now the British tunnellers had their greatest success. It had taken them six months to tunnel under the German front line on the Messines Ridge – one tunnel was nearly a kilometre long. They laid 19 mines and on 7 June detonated them. The explosion, which was felt in Britain, was described as "a strange early morning shock, like an earthquake". It killed 10,000 Germans and 8,000 more were taken prisoner.

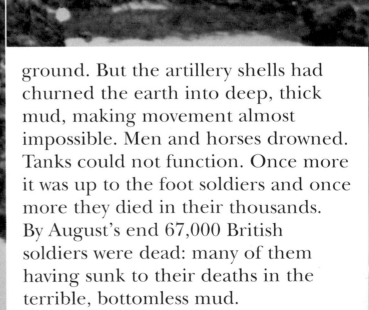

Landscape from Hell – the battlefield at Passchendaele in October 1917.

Passchendaele

Surely one more offensive would end the war. The British had broken through at Ypres, but delays and rain bogged them down. On 31 July the British artillery opened up and the Allied advance on the Passchendaele ridge began. Amazingly, it gained ground. But the artillery shells had churned the earth into deep, thick mud, making movement almost impossible. Men and horses drowned. Tanks could not function. Once more it was up to the foot soldiers and once more they died in their thousands. By August's end 67,000 British soldiers were dead: many of them having sunk to their deaths in the terrible, bottomless mud.

YANKS IN ACTION

When General Pershing received a telegram in April 1917 asking how well he spoke French, he had no idea that he would be put in charge of the US Army in Europe.

He spoke French quite well, so he was given the job. Then he had to get his army across the Atlantic, which took some organising. When the American troops first arrived they did not form a separate force but were attached to British and French units.

Four battalions of Black American soldiers were incorporated into the French army. Nobody believed the Americans would be any good: they had not been to war before, while the soldiers they fought alongside were hard-bitten veterans who by now had seen it all. At first, the Germans, too, were not impressed.

But the doubters were wrong. By September 1918 there were more than three million American soldiers in France and they were making their presence felt. By the end of the war, nearly 50,000 "doughboys", as they were called, had been killed.

● US troops go into action in France, May 1918.

ACTION ELSEWHERE

The war was not restricted to France and eastern Europe. There was equally intense fighting elsewhere.

The Italian campaign

For four years a very bitter war had raged in the north of Italy as German and Austrian troops tried to break through the Alps and invade Italy. Italian troops with French, British and later American help tried to repel them in cruel battles that raged remorselessly to and fro across difficult terrain over mountains and in river valleys.

● These photographs were taken by a German officer on campaign in Russia, Bulgaria and Salonika.

Salonika

In October 1915 French and British troops landed at this port in north-east Greece to help the Serbs. It was a hopeless campaign: a huge army was stuck, racked by disease in what the French General Sarrail called his "concentration camp". Salonika was destroyed – accidentally, by fire – before the Allies could withdraw.

Palestine

The Allies fought a long campaign against the Turks and Germans in Palestine before General Allenby drove them out of Jerusalem in December 1917. At last the Arabs were free of Turkish domination. But Arthur Balfour, the British Foreign Secretary, had already issued his famous declaration: that there should one day be a Jewish homeland in Palestine. Our modern world was taking shape.

1918

With Russia now out of the war the Central Powers turned all their strength against Britain, France and America. But Germany had suffered crippling losses. There was one hope left – a lightning advance through Allied lines to reach Paris.

In March 1918 the German army struck, pushing the Allies back. By May the Allies were further back than when the trenches were first dug in 1914. In the British bases behind the lines clerks and typists were given guns and told to be ready to defend themselves. It must be the end: on some days the Germans advanced 16 kilometres. By June they were on the River Marne again, 90 kilometres from Paris.

German troops go into action during the spring offensive of 1918.

Even in the darkest days of the war, life went on. A German non-commissioned officer has his photo taken with his wife while on a few days' leave, 1918.

Australians and Canadians headed the assault: the German army crumbled before them. Later Ludendorff wrote "8 August was the black day of the German army."

"What do you war-prolongers want?" exhausted German soldiers asked of new reinforcements going up to the front. The tide of the war had turned, for the last time.

"Our backs to the wall"

On 11 April Haig gave a famous Order of the Day. "Victory will belong to the side that holds out longest . . . With our backs to the wall and believing in the justice of our cause each one of us must fight to the end."

And they did. All through summer the battle raged – and gradually, very gradually, the Allies gained the upper hand. The Germans could get no further west than the River Marne – their attack on Paris never happened. Reinforcements and new big guns arrived. On 8 August British troops once again went "over the top" at the Somme. But this time, there was no mistake. Preparations had been made secretly – this time the enemy had no idea what was to come.

In Flanders fields

In Flanders fields the poppies blow
Between the crosses, row on row
That mark our place; and in the sky
The larks, still bravely singing, fly
Scarce heard amid the guns below.

We are the Dead. Short days ago
We lived, felt dawn, saw sunset glow,
Loved and were loved, and now we lie
in Flanders fields.

Take up our quarrel with the foe:
To you from failing hands we throw
The torch; be yours to hold it high
If ye break faith with us who die
We shall not sleep, though poppies grow
In Flanders fields.

John McCrae (1872-1918)

ADVANCE AT LAST

Now the movement was all one way. Kaiser Wilhelm knew that his great ambitions for Germany had failed. His army was cracking.

The Americans were fresh, the British better equipped and the French had new hope. In September a new offensive began: British, French and American troops advanced together. Steadily, the Germans were driven back.

● British troops trudge past a huge flooded shell crater on the Western Front.

The Saint-Quentin Canal

Hidden by fog and using rafts, ladders and life-belts, British troops crossed the Saint-Quentin canal on the Western Front, took 5,000 prisoners, huge numbers of guns, advanced nearly six kilometres and overran the Hindenburg Line. This victory was a huge morale booster. The way to Berlin seemed open.

The final throes

Only stubbornness could delay the end. German troops fought on tenaciously. The Austrian army was crumbling fast. Many of their soldiers were Slavs, who began refusing to fight the Serbs.

Germany turned to desperate measures. The German High Seas Fleet was ordered to sea for one last all-or-nothing fight against the British: the sailors refused to go. Mutiny spread. The red flag of Bolshevism flew from town halls all over Germany. Germany, it seemed, was about to have its own revolution. Meanwhile the Allies continued their advance on the Western Front: on 4 November the British attacked the Sambre Canal. While organising a crossing on rafts, Wilfred Owen, the greatest war poet of all, was killed.

In Germany, the Kaiser was wondering what he should do. He had led his country into war; now he saw its inevitable ruin. On 9 November he abdicated and fled to Holland.

On 10 November Canadian and British troops re-entered Mons, where the British had started four years before. Still the German soldiers would not give in. An officer noted that three of the British killed that day wore the 1914 medal – their deaths seemed the more bitter so nearly had they survived the war.

THE BITTER END

On 11 November the Armistice, which had taken more than a month to negotiate, was signed. Meanwhile thousands more men had died. Allied troops now occupied Germany as far as the Rhine and Germany had to give up land and possessions.

Germany's prized High Seas Fleet was taken to Scapa Flow in Scotland. After four terrible years it was at last quiet on the Western Front. The opposing armies were worn out. But Germany's humiliation had only just started.

"What's an armistice, mate?" a British soldier asked. "Time to bury the dead," another answered.

All over Europe people celebrated the end of the war with joy, as here in Paris in 1918.

The aftermath – 'flu

Death in war had, for the time being, stopped. But another sort of death was creeping across Europe. In an age without antibiotics, an influenza epidemic meant certain death – and now perhaps the worst such epidemic ever known began ravaging Europe. It struck millions whose resistance, after years of short rations and poor nourishment, was very low. It could not have come at a worse time. In Britain alone, 150,000 people died in 1919, including some who had fought and survived all the horrors of the war.

Counting the dead

Nobody knows quite how many people were killed in this war. One thing is clear: with "only" roughly a million servicemen killed, Britain and her Empire got off more lightly than almost any other major combatant. Russia had probably lost three million – nobody knows for certain. Almost a million and a half Frenchmen had been killed. Nearly two million Germans died, more than a million Austro-Hungarians and two million Turks. Italy lost nearly half a million men.

Add to these the wounded, unable now to lead proper lives, and the hosts of prisoners and the effect was the loss of almost an entire generation.

All governments handed out medals during the war. From left to right: German Iron Cross, British War Medal, British Victory Medal.

"The Armistice was timed to commence at 11 am on 11 November and till that hour there was heavy firing from the German lines. A German machine gun remained in action the whole morning opposite our lines. Just before 11 am, a thousand rounds were fired from it in a practically ceaseless burst. At five minutes to eleven the machine gunner got up, took off his hat to us, and walked away.

"At 11 am there came a great cheering from the German lines; and the village church bells rang. But on our side there were only a few shouts. I had heard more for a rum ration. The match was over; it had been a damned bad game."

A British colonel describes the end of the war on the Western Front

NEVER AGAIN?

"The War to end all wars". It must, everybody agreed, never happen again. "Hang the Kaiser," some said. But what would that achieve?

Germany started the war, so Germany must accept full responsibility and pay. At the same time, it must be made quite certain that Germany could never fight again and break the peace of Europe. A great Peace Conference was arranged for 1919 at Versailles, near Paris. The Allies had two main ideas, one good, one bad.

Versailles

The good idea was President Wilson's "League of Nations". But it was given no powers and could not stop the terrible events of World War Two 20 years later. It would, however, lead to the formation of the United Nations.

The bad idea

Seared by the war, French President Georges Clemenceau and British Prime Minister Lloyd George insisted on Germany's abject humiliation. It was to lose territory. In the east large parts were given to Czechoslavakia and Poland. In the west France got Alsace-Lorraine back. Allied troops would be stationed on the Rhine. Germany could not rebuild its armed forces and had to give up all its weapons. It also had to pay reparations to the victorious powers which would cripple the country for years.

The signing of the Treaty of Versailles, as depicted in a painting by British artist Sir William Orpen.

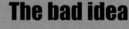

DENMARK

GREAT BRITAIN

NETHERLANDS

BELGIUM

Ruhr

GERMANY

EAST PRUSSIA

Land ceded to Poland

RUSSIA

POLAND

CZECHOSLOVAKIA

Alsace-Lorraine to France

SWITZERLAND

AUSTRIA

HUNGARY

ROMANIA

FRANCE

ITALY

At first the Germans refused to sign because they would not accept the idea of "war guilt". But in the end an event occurred that made the Allies determined that Germany would sign.

"The stain of surrender"

One thing all Germans were sure of: their forces had never been defeated in battle; their leaders had merely decided to stop the war. Many Germans regarded this as an act of betrayal.

But what about the ships of the German High Seas Fleet, now at the British deep-water base in Scapa Flow? By the terms of the Treaty of Versailles they belonged to the Allies. Not so, said their prisoner crews.

On 21 June 1919 the German ships were scuttled by their own crews, and one by one they sank. As a result no one would ever be able to say that the German Navy had surrendered.

The Allies were furious. They insisted that Germany sign the Treaty of Versailles. But, by doing so, they almost guaranteed a Second World War with Germany.

"We are required to admit that we alone are war guilty; such an admission on my lips would be a lie ."

Count Brockdorff-Rantzau, senior German delegate at Versailles

A TRAGIC LEGACY

For four years all classes and types of people had been united in war. But when it was over the bad old ways came back. Unemployment, poverty, near-starvation for some, ex-soldiers begging, a General Strike – had nobody learned anything?

The war cemeteries of Europe are permanent memorials to the thousands who died. This picture shows a British cemetery near Ypres, Belgium.

That was in Britain. In Germany, things were far, far worse. Inflation was so great that it took a wheelbarrow to carry enough banknotes to buy a bar of chocolate. Unemployment was appalling and the entire German people felt a rising tide of grievance. They wanted their lost lands back; they wanted reunion with fellow Germans in East Prussia; they wanted the Allies out of the Rhineland. Above all they wanted the world to remember that their armies had never been defeated in battle.

When Adolf Hitler and his National Socialist Party took office in 1933 promising to recapture Germany's lost glory, it was as a direct result of what had been forced on them at Versailles. The aim of the Treaty was to ensure Germany never went to war again. The result was the opposite.

Not again...

In 1939 the Second World War started and in 1945 it ended in another defeat for Germany and its allies. But it had been even more destructive than the first war and left an infinitely more dangerous world behind it. So what lessons could be learned this time?

"Be magnanimous in victory," said British Prime Minister Winston Churchill. This time Germany was helped to rebuild and brought back among the world's nations. Over the years there have been public reconciliations, the most famous being that between France and Germany at Verdun in 1984. Most importantly, the United Nations Organization was set up, this time with real powers.

Building a better Europe

In Europe, the question was how to stop the continent's many countries erupting into war as they had from time to time for over 1,000 years?

The answer seemed to be "If you can't beat them, join them," and gradually, the European Union was set up. The Union may be flawed and inefficient and sometimes even undermine national freedoms, but it is the only way of uniting states which have been traditional enemies so closely that they never go to war with each other again.

The humiliation of Germany in the First World War led to the rise of Adolf Hitler.

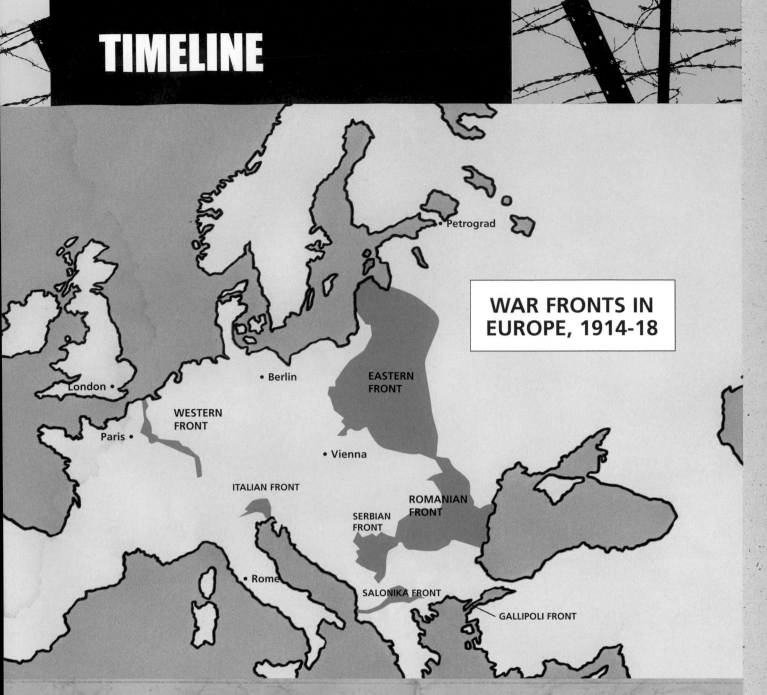

WAR FRONTS IN EUROPE, 1914-18

- Petrograd
- London
- Berlin
- EASTERN FRONT
- WESTERN FRONT
- Paris
- Vienna
- ITALIAN FRONT
- ROMANIAN FRONT
- SERBIAN FRONT
- Rome
- SALONIKA FRONT
- GALLIPOLI FRONT

1914

28 June Assassination of Archduke Ferdinand in Sarajevo: **28 July** Austria declares war on Serbia; **2 August** Germany declares war on Russia; **3 August** France declares war on Germany; **4 August** German troops enter Belgium. Britain declares war on Germany; Germans advance in West against French and British. Russians advance in East on Germany and Austria; Turkey joins Central powers;
23 August BEF repels German troops at Mons. Japan joins war on Allied side;
29 August Battle of Tannenberg. Germans defeat Russians and halt advance.

5-6 September Battle of the Marne. French and British halt German advance on Paris; "Race to the Sea" ensues; **17-31 October** First Battle of Ypres. French and British stop all German advances. Trench system established from English Channel to Switzerland.

1915

January Kitchener's "New Army" totals 1,200,000 volunteers, now in training.
10-13 March Battle of Neuve Chapelle. British offensive. Few gains, 13,000 lost.
22 April Start of Second Battle of Ypres. Germans use poison gas for first time.

25 April Australian, New Zealand, Indian, French and British forces land at Gallipoli. Soon reaches stalemate; **3 May** Italy enters war on Allied side; **7 May** RMS *Lusitania* torpedoed by U-boat; **8 May** 2nd Battle of Ypres ends in stalemate. Over 120,000 men from all sides lost; **8 May** French attack at Battle of Artois; **4 August** Warsaw, Poland, falls to Germans; **6 August** Gallipoli campaign. Allied landings at Suvla Bay. Stalemate; **6 September** Bulgaria enters war on side of Central Powers; **25 September** First Battle of Loos begins. 800,000 French and British troops advance on Germans. No gains. Allies lose 250,000 men, Germans 200,000; **19/20 December** Allied forces withdrawn from Suvla Bay.

1916

21 February Battle for Verdun opens with German artillery bombardment; **25 February** Verdun: Germans capture Fort Douaumont. Pétain takes command of French troops; **10 April** Verdun: French repel Germans from Mort-Homme Hill; **13 May** Jutland. British and German fleets clash. Neither wins battle outright; **15 May** Austrians attack Italy through Alps. Italians repel them; **4 June** Russians attack and destroy most of Austrian front line; **9 June** Verdun: Germans capture Fort de Vaux; **21 June** Verdun: Germans fire 100,000 phosgene gas shells; **1 July** British start offensive at River Somme. Appalling first day casualties. No gains made; **11 July** Germans halt Verdun offensive. French go on attack; **27 September** Somme: British take Thiepval; **11 October** Verdun: French retake Fort Douaumont; **13 November** Somme: British take Beaumont-Hamel; **1 December** Battle of Somme ends. British lose 415,000, French 195,000, Germans probably 600,000; **18 December** Battle of Verdun ends. French and Germans each lose 350,000 men; Germans retire to new positions and start building the Hindenburg Line. Worst winter for 30 years sets in.

1917

17 January Zimmermann Telegram intercepted and decoded; **8 March** Food riots in Russian city of Petrograd; **15 March** Czar Nicholas abdicates; **6 April** US declares war on Central Powers; **9 April** Battle of Arras starts. Canadians assault Vimy Ridge; **13 April** French attack beaten back with huge losses; **3 May** French soldiers refuse to fight – mutiny starts; **7 June** British mine Messines Ridge. Huge German loss of life; **1 July** Russians attack on Eastern Front: Germans beat them back. Russia now in no state to fight further; **31 July** British advance with infantry and tanks. Appalling losses in mud. Germans slowly pushed back; **9 October** Battle of Passchendaele opens; **October** Bolshevik Revolution in Russia. Lenin takes power. Russia out of the war; **22 October** Austrians and Germans attack Italians at Caporetto; **12 November** Battle of Passchendaele ends; **20 November** British tanks in action at Cambrai. First-ever successful tank battle; **30 November** Germans counter-attack; **9 December** British General Allenby enters Jerusalem.

1918

21 March Germans begin advance on Western Front; **28 March** Advance fizzles out. **9 April** Germans try again. British lose 240,000 men in forty days; **27 May** Germans break through British lines; **June-July** Allies fight back. Americans take significant part in fighting; **August** Allied advance continues. **8 August** British attack at the Somme again. This time they succeed; **August** German morale begins to crack; **26 September** Battle of St Quentin Canal; **29 September** Allies break through Hindenburg Line; **1 October** Allenby defeats Turks at Megiddo; **29 October** German Navy mutinies; **30 October** Turkey signs Armistice; **3 November** Austria signs Armistice; **9 November** Kaiser Wilhelm abdicates; **11 November** Fighting stops at 11 am. Armistice signed. War over.

GLOSSARY

Armistice Agreement between two warring sides to stop fighting so talks about peace can take place. An "armistice" usually means the end of war; a "ceasefire" is only a pause.

Artillery The big guns used in warfare on land. Placed behind the trenches, their fire was concentrated on the enemy's positions until the infantry advanced on them.

Austria-Hungary The united country, of which Austria was the senior partner, which was the centre of the Austro-Hungarian Empire ruled from Vienna by the Hapsburg family. Germany's main ally in the First World War.

Battalion A unit of about a thousand soldiers which formed part of a larger unit, the regiment.

Blockade When a navy patrols the sea to prevent supplies from reaching the enemy. The British Royal Navy blockaded German ports during the First World War.

Bolshevism Better known as Communism. The idea, put forward by Karl Marx, that power should belong to the people. Vladimir Lenin led the Russian Bolshevik Revolution in 1917. Bolshevism influenced Germany in 1918.

Bombardment Concentrated shelling by the artillery. Most bombardments in the First World War came before an infantry advance.

Chancellor German equivalent of Prime Minister.

Convoy Group of merchant ships sailing together and escorted by warships to protect them from attack by U-boats.

Court-martial A military court, in which a soldier is tried by officers for breaking military law.

Dreadnought The Royal Navy's "super-battleship", with more armour and firepower than any others.

Entente Cordiale The informal agreement between Britain and France ending centuries of hostility and ensuring that they were allies in the First World War.

Firestep Ridge along the front of a trench which enabled soldiers to fire at the enemy while remaining under cover.

Infantry Foot soldiers; they bore the brunt of the fighting in the First World War and made all the advances across no-man's land to the enemy trenches.

Intelligence The art of finding out the enemy's intentions. It has two functions: gathering evidence through means such as spies and codebreaking, and interpreting that evidence.

Mills bomb A hand grenade, a small bomb that can be carried and thrown. It was the most efficient of many such bombs. The German canister bomb, a tin can packed with gunpowder, wadding and nails was a similar type of bomb.

Mine A large bomb left in a particular place, either to explode when it is touched – such as a naval or land mine – or buried at the end of a long tunnel to be detonated at a set time, as at Messines Ridge in 1917.

Mutiny A revolt by soldiers or sailors against their officers. The most serious mutinies in the First World War were by the French and Russians. British soldiers mutinied at Etaples, near Boulogne, and German soldiers and sailors mutinied towards the end of the war.

Parapet The protective barrier at the front of a trench, often made from sandbags.

Patriotism Love of one's country – a quality much devalued in the First World War.

Reconnaissance Watching the enemy's positions to gain knowledge of their troop movements.

Reparations What a defeated power has to give to make up to the victors for what they have lost.

Respirator A mask worn during a gas attack to enable the wearer to breathe without inhaling the gas. Often called a "gas mask".

Shell, shelling A shell is a large bullet fired by the big guns of the artillery. Shelling is the act of firing them.

Treaty A binding agreement between two or more nations. The First World War was inevitable because of all the different countries' treaty obligations to each other; it was ended by the Treaty of Versailles.

Trenches The deep ditches dug in the ground which were the main feature of the Western Front during the First World War. The trenches of the opposing sides stretched from the Belgian coast to Switzerland.

U-boat German submarine. "U" stands for *untersee* (undersea).

Volunteer A person who does something, such as joining the armed forces, of his or her own free will. "Conscripts" join the services when they are forced to, or "conscripted".

INDEX